A

SELF

MADE

OF

WORDS

Date: 4/30/14

808.02 KLA
Klaus, Carl H.,
A self made of words :
crafting a distinctive persona

CARL H. KLAUS

A SELF MADE OF WORDS

CRAFTING A DISTINCTIVE PERSONA IN NONFICTION WRITING

UNIVERSITY OF IOWA PRESS   Iowa City

University of Iowa Press, Iowa City 52242

Copyright © 2013 by Carl H. Klaus

www.uiowapress.org

Printed in the United States of America

Design by Richard Hendel

The University of Iowa Press is a member of Green Press Initiative and is committed to preserving natural resources.

Printed on acid-free paper

Library of Congress Cataloging-in-Publication Data
Klaus, Carl H.
A self made of words: crafting a distinctive persona in nonfiction writing / by Carl H. Klaus.
pages cm
Includes bibliographical references.
ISBN-13: 978-1-60938-194-3, 1-60938-194-7 (pbk.)
ISBN-13: 978-1-60938-214-8, 1-60938-214-5 (ebook)
1. Persona (Literature) 2. Essay—Authorship—Problems, exercises, etc. 3. Self in literature. I. Title.
PN218.K56 2013
808.02—dc23   2013007552

To ROBERT SCHOLES

With gratitude

for teaching me the value of a little book

and showing me how to write one

Never to be yourself, and yet always;

that is the problem.

— Virginia Woolf, "The Modern Essay"

CONTENTS

This book is devoted to your self and the ways you can bring it to life in writing. The idea of doing such a work came to mind shortly after I finished *The Made-Up Self* in 2010 and discovered that there wasn't a book in print on the specifics of how to create a distinctive self—a crucial element in writing, strangely overlooked. So I spent the last few years putting together the ideas and suggestions I've gathered and developed over the course of my work as an author, editor, and teacher of nonfiction.

Though you can't see it on the page, an impression of your self is there in everything you write, and it's bound to influence the way that readers respond to your work. That being the case, it's best to take charge of how you come across in your prose so that you create an engaging impression, rather than letting your written self take shape haphazardly in a form, style, or voice that might misrepresent you or turn off your readers. To help you avoid that risk and create a distinctive self, I've focused this book on the most important way of projecting your self in nonfiction prose—by means of a "persona," which is a version of your self made of words, a carefully crafted version that you can vary as you see fit. Confident or fretful, solemn or sassy, tough or tender, casual or formal—these are just a few of the many stances you can assume. So many options, it might seem like a mere gesture to come across as you wish. But every persona is the byproduct of numerous decisions made in the process of writing—decisions about what to say and how to say it. Though any single word or phrase or sentence might seem to make little difference in the way you come across, collectively they produce an impression of who you are or seem to be. Thus it's all the more important to consider the various ways to create an engaging and distinctive persona.

To help you achieve that goal, I've divided this book into two parts: an introduction to the nature and function of a persona, which includes some preliminary exercises, and a survey of the most important elements of writing, from point of view and organization to diction and sentence structure, with exercises that will give you practice in using each element to create a persona of your choice.

}

PART I
YOUR SELF
IN WRITING

Your self in writing? Yes, if you wrote it, you must be in it somehow, for an imprint of your self is unavoidable, as surely as a fingerprint. It's there in the gist of what you say and the style of how you say it. Overtly in a personal essay or opinion piece. Implicitly in an article or a report. The only problem is that a version of your self made of words, a persona, is not really the same as your flesh and blood self. No matter how genuine you might think it sounds, your written self is an illusion, a stand-in for you. And since it's made of words, your persona can be made to sound any way you want. Indeed, you can make such different versions of your persona that they might seem to be written by distinctly different persons, as you'll see in the following pages. But that's not surprising when you realize that we all have so many sides that a single unchanging persona couldn't really do justice to the complexity of our lives and of our selves.

} YOUR SELF AND YOUR PERSONA

To see how varied one's persona can be, I'd like you to reread the preceding paragraph, which is addressed to "you" in an informal style; then compare the way I sound in that passage with the way I would have come across in a completely different style, beginning instead with a long impersonal sentence and a scattering of big words, without any mention of "you":

> The persona embodied in a piece of written discourse has so frequently been considered an authentic manifestation of its author's self that the illusory and artificially crafted nature of it has often been overlooked.

Or consider how differently I'd sound if I'd written it in a personal and colloquial style, using plain and simple language, focusing primarily on thoughts about my writing and yours:

> The way I write is so much a part of me, a reflection of who I am, that I figure it must be the same with everyone else. I mean, who's there in your writing if not you?

{3

Or imagine how I might have come across if I had started out in first-person plural and tried something in a metaphorical vein:

> Our writing so often seems to be a reflection of ourselves, or some facet of ourselves, that it's tempting to think our prose is a mirror, when it might in fact be a hall of mirrors, giving readers a very distorted image of ourselves.

Given such different personae, you might wonder which is the most authentic, which one closest to the real me. And my answer would be that each one reflects an important aspect of my self: the metaphorical one embodies my literary inclinations, the casual one my impulsive side, the impersonal one my longtime academic experience, and the opening one in direct address to "you" echoes my desire to engage in a friendly give-and-take with you. So in a way they're all reflective of me, yet none of them encompasses all the dimensions of my self, and therefore none of them is fully true to me. All of us, in fact, have so many different sides that no single form of writing, no single style or voice, could do justice to our selves. Thus, the more versatile we can be in our writing, the more likely we are to be true at least to some aspect or side of our selves at any particular moment in our lives. Right now, for example, another variation on the theme of my opening paragraph has just come to mind, embodying an important point of view that isn't reflected in any of the others, so I've included it here:

> Me and my persona — we've been together so long it's sometimes hard to tell us apart. Or so it might

4}

seem to someone who doesn't really know either of us. But I do, and I can tell you it's changed so much, as have I, that I sometimes wonder whether we have anything to do with each other at all.

Though the opening sentence of this passage sounds like the earlier one in first person singular, it also calls into question the breezy equation of self and persona that permeates the earlier passage, and thus reflects the changeableness that I perceive both in my self and my persona — changeableness that is to some extent inevitable in all of us.

PERSONA AND PERFORMANCE

Another way to think about your persona is to consider it an essential element in a performance of sorts. To take part in a performance may seem like a fanciful — and somewhat devious — thing to do in your writing. But most of us perform a variety of roles every day of our lives, given the different people we encounter — at one moment with friends, at another with the boss, at another with colleagues, at another with loved ones. With each of them, we tend to behave and talk in a somewhat different way, presenting a different version of ourselves, a different persona, that resonates both with them and with a distinctive aspect of ourselves. And we change not only because of the person(s) at hand but also because of our mood or the gist of what we're saying. So it's not at all far-fetched to think we might do the same thing in our writing. Or, as E. B. White says, the essayist can "be any sort of person, according to his mood or his subject matter — philosopher, scold, jester, raconteur, confidant, pundit, devil's advocate, enthusiast."

The ability to adopt a changing persona is essential not only to writing effective essays but also to producing such varied kinds of writing as personal letters, blogs, technical reports, newsletters, opinion pieces, and analyses. And the practice of adapting one's persona to such varied prose has a long and distinguished history, as you can see from the following passages, all by Benjamin Franklin:

(1) About this time I met with an odd volume of *The Spectator*. It was the third. I had never before seen any of them. I bought it, read it over and over, and was much delighted with it. I thought the writing excellent, and wished if possible, to imitate it.

(2) Be studious in your profession, and you will be learned. Be industrious and frugal, and you will be rich. Be sober and temperate, and you will be healthy. Be in general virtuous, and you will be happy.

(3) There is in every village a vacant dwelling, called the strangers' house. Here they are placed, while the old men go round from hut to hut, acquainting the inhabitants that strangers are arrived, who are probably hungry and weary; and everyone sends them what he can spare of victuals; and skins to repose on.

Each of these pieces stands out from the others not only because of its content but also because of its point of view and style—each so distinctive they could have been written by three different people. The first one, from Franklin's autobiography, is marked by its very personal manner, by the predominance of "I," also by its plain diction and relatively short sentences, as if its author were as frank and unassuming as the style of his personal account. The second passage, by contrast, is very stylized, each sentence in the imperative mode, the voice of command, each sentence tersely phrased in the manner of an aphorism, and each sentence balanced in the same way to emphasize a cause-and-effect morality, as if its author were a very self-confident preacher or teacher. A persona that Franklin evidently felt free to assume, given that in this case he was concluding a letter to a young man who had solicited his opinion on early marriages. The third passage, on the other hand, has neither the plain personal manner of the first nor the authoritarian style of the second. Instead, its third-person point of view and matter-of-fact style, describing village behavior in a lengthy and detailed sentence, creates the impresssion of having been written by an objective observer, somewhat like a latter-day cultural anthropologist, a stance that Franklin must have wanted to assume in this instance because he was writing a pamphlet attempting to dispel the prejudices of colonial Americans about the native American Indians. So the content, point of view, and style of each passage project a different self created by Franklin to meet a complex set of circumstances existing as much outside him as within him.

If changing styles and stances seem to compromise a writer's integrity, consider the folly of ignoring such adaptive behavior—imagine Franklin writing about the Indians in the personal mode of his autobiography. It would be as inappropriate as attending a public meeting in a bathrobe. Each set of conditions calls for a different form, style, or point of view, and our response had best come within its boundaries if we hope to be effective. The boundaries are not narrow; they often allow for a range of voices, enabling each of us to authenticate ourselves. Franklin, for example, needn't have concluded his letter in such an aphoristic style, but evidently he felt moved to do so, and the situation also gave him the liberty to do so. So it might be said that effective writing is the result of a complex interaction between our private intentions and the public circumstances of communication.

Changing subject matter as well as changing circumstances also produce changing personae, as you can see by looking at two more passages, in this case by the contemporary essayist and film writer, Nora Ephron:

(1) We have lived through the era when happiness was a warm puppy, and the era when happiness was a dry martini, and now we have come to the era when happiness is "knowing what your uterus looks like."

(2) I broke up with Bill a long time ago. It's always hard to remember love — years pass and you say to yourself, Was I really in love, or was I just kidding myself?

These passages, like the ones by Benjamin Franklin, sound so different from each other that it seems as if they could have been written by different authors. In part, of course, the contrast is produced by striking differences in the style of each passage: the first one distinguished by its carefully crafted three-part series in closely parallel form ("the era when . . . the era when . . . the era when . . ."), whereas the second, by contrast, appears to be so casual as not to have been crafted at all, as if Ephron were talking out her thoughts as they came to mind without any revision. But those differences are a reflection of the different content in each passage — the first, an overview of three different cultural periods, the second a bit of reminiscence about an emotional breakup (which actually refers to her disillusionment with Bill Clinton), a reminiscence that leads to reflections about the uncertainty of love. But the casualness of the second is probably as deliberate as the careful crafting of the first.

CONTENT, PURPOSE, AND PERSONA

Though most of this book is focused on the form of your writing, on how to word things and how to organize and present your material, it's important to keep in mind the rhetorical truth exemplified in the passages by Ephron and Franklin — that the content and purpose of a person's writing exert a major influence on the character of a person's written self. An autobiography, after all, is sure to call forth a different persona from a letter of advice or a field report. So too, a piece about changing cultural eras is likely to evoke a different persona from a piece about an emotional breakup (personal or political). But beyond such obvious differences, the persona in a specific piece of writing is also influenced by its author's distinctive slant on things, by thoughts and feelings that are expressed or implied, by details that are emphasized or downplayed — in other words, by the specific content of the piece. For example, if you look again at the first paragraph of this book and the four alternative versions of it that I produced, you'll see that each version has a somewhat different concern from the others. Whereas the first version confidently asserts the difference between a person's written self and his or her flesh-and-blood self, the second version worries about the mistaken tendency of people to confuse one self with the other, while the third version proclaims the identity of both selves, the fourth version ponders the causes and possible effects of the tendency to confuse one self with the other, and the fifth version focuses on the changeability of both my self and my persona. In other words, the different versions not only embody different sides of myself, but they also reflect some of my different thoughts on the relationship of a persona to its author, and those differing thoughts give rise to a different persona in each case.

The nature of a persona is rarely a simple matter: it's the byproduct of several influences, and it can change markedly, even in the course of a single piece, as in "My Father, My Fiction," a personal essay by Joyce Carol Oates. As its title suggests, Oates's essay focuses on her father and the profound connection of his life story to the nature of her fiction writing. Here is an excerpt from Oates's biographical account of her father:

> My father was born in 1914 in Lockport, N.Y., a small city approximately 20 miles north of Buffalo and 15 miles south of Lake Ontario, in Niagara County; its distinctive feature is the steep rock-sided Erie Canal that runs literally through its core. Because they were poor, my grandmother (the former Blanche Morganstern) frequently moved with her son from one low-priced rental to another. But after he grew up and married my mother (the former Carolina Bush), my father came to live in my mother's adoptive parents' farmhouse in Millersport; and he has remained on that land ever since.

This passage about Oates's father stands out not only because of its attention to the poverty of his circumstances but also because of its informational tenor from start to finish. Oates's style here is so matter-of-fact, so free of emotional overtones, that she sounds like an objective biographer rather than an admiring or affectionate or sympathetic daughter. So it might well be inferred that the way she comes across here is the result of a deliberate decision not to display her feelings in this passage about her father — and/or to let the facts speak for themselves. Whatever the case, a passage such as this one clearly embodies a central truth about writing — specifically, that no matter whom you're writing about, whether it's your father, a friend, or a person you've never met before, you're also conveying something about yourself by the way you choose to write about that other person. Imagine, for example, how differently Oates would have come across if she had begun the paragraph cited above by asserting that "the pitiable circumstances of my father began when he was a little child in Lockport, N.Y."

Oates's intent to provide a dispassionate account of things pertaining to her father and mother is also evident in a passage that comes several paragraphs later, about the farm that they shared with her maternal grandparents:

> Facts: the property my parents shared with my Bush grandparents was a small farm with a fruit orchard, some cherry trees, some apple trees, primarily Bartlett pears. My memories are of chickens, Rhode Island reds, pecking obsessively in the dirt. . . . Fruit picking, epecially the harvest of hundreds of bushel baskets of pears, fell to my father, when he wasn't working in Lockport at Harrison Radiator.

The latter part of this passsage also bears witness, though without comment, to the burdensome quality of her father's life. But the full significance of this and Oates's other informational passages only becomes clear a couple of short paragraphs later when she directly expresses her thoughts and feelings in a different style and tenor:

> I wonder if it is evident how painfully difficult it has been for me to write this seemingly informal memoir? — as if I were staring into a dazzling beacon of light, yet expected to see?
>
> All children mythologize their parents, who are to them after all giants of the landscape of early childhood; and I'm sure I am no exception.
>
> And yet . . . and yet: it does seem to me that my parents are remarkable people, both in themselves as persons, as "personalities," and as representatives and survivors of a world so harsh and so repetitive in its harshness as to defy evocation, except perhaps in art.

In these and succeeding paragraphs Oates is as forthright about her thoughts and feelings as she had been reticent about them before, openly expressing not only her anguish about the harsh circumstances of her parents' lives but also her admiration of their endurance in the face of those circumstances. Given her reticence in the passages I've cited, as well as the fluency of her prose in those passages, I imagine that many if not most readers will have been surprised to learn "how painfully difficult it [had] been for [her] to write this seemingly informal memoir." Thus the revelation of her thoughts and feelings is all the more dramatic given her previous suppression of them.

Now that you've seen how effective it can be to project a dispassionately informational manner followed by a direct revelation of your thoughts and feelings, I'd like you to write a few paragraphs about your father and/or mother, or some other important person in your life. In the first couple of paragraphs, your aim should be to write about them in as matter-of-fact and dispassionate a style as possible; in the next couple of paragraphs, your aim should be to write about them as frankly as possible. After you've finished this assignment, I'd like you to write a separate paragraph reflecting on what you discovered from trying out these different styles and stances.

SELF-REVELATION AND SELF-CREATION

Though I've written about self-revelation in Oates and other essayists, and have discussed this fascinating subject in writing courses, I've never tried to offer guidance about it in a how-to book such as this. So I'm a bit uneasy about discussing it here, especially because self-revelation involves issues of privacy that individual persons have to decide for themselves. After all, only you can determine what you're willing to reveal about your private thoughts and feelings. Yet self-revelation is so important an element in creating and projecting your self that I can hardly ignore it. As an example of what I mean, just consider how differently you'd perceive me and how differently you'd think about what I'm saying here had I not begun this part with the five sentences you've just finished reading, but had begun instead like this:

> Self-revelation is such a crucial element in creating and projecting your self that you can hardly avoid it. But given that each person's sense of privacy is a deeply personal matter, only you can decide how much you're willing to reveal about the drift of your private thoughts about yourself.

This two-sentence opening reveals nothing whatsoever of my private thoughts about writing this little segment of the book, whereas the previous five-sentence paragraph frankly divulges my uneasiness in writing it. Likewise, the two-sentence version is addressed to "you," whereas the five-sentence opening is dominantly in the first-person "I." So the two-sentence version projects the persona of a straightforward, no-nonsense expounder of the subject at hand, whereas the five-sentence version embodies the persona of a somewhat self-conscious and fretful author. Your reaction to these different versions will probably depend to some extent on your rhetorical preferences: if you prefer that authors stick to ideas without talking about themselves, you'll be inclined to prefer the two-sentence version, but if you're receptive to authors sharing private thoughts that might be relevant to the subject at hand, you might prefer the five-sentence version. Whatever your preference, there's no denying that my decision to be self-revelatory in this instance enables me not only to highlight the difference between self-revelation and self-restraint but also to show how self-revelation can be used to create a distinctive persona, as it does in the case of Oates's essay.

So before you read any further, I'd like you to write a short piece about a memorable experience that sticks in your mind clearly enough that you're not only able to remember what happened in vivid detail but are also willing to reveal some of the thoughts and feelings you had, either in the course of that experience or that you now have in the process of remembering it and writing about it. Choose an incident important enough to you that you're willing to keep writing about it, and revising what you've written, during the various exercises that follow. When you finish your piece, I'd also like you to write a brief commentary on it, noting the problems you encountered in recalling and writing about the experience, as well as taking account of any thoughts about the experience that came to your mind in the process of writing about it. As an example of what I have in mind, here is a piece that I wrote for this assignment about a memorable experience of my own, followed by a brief commentary on it:

On a midwinter evening, some five years ago, after getting into bed and resting my head on the pillow, I noticed the room beginning to move a bit to the right, but then the movement increased, speeding up until the room was spinning so rapidly I soon felt as dizzy as if my body itself had been spinning. I tried to resist the movement by focusing on the dresser across from my bed, but the dresser, like the picture hanging above it, was also moving in unison with the room.

Never having experienced such a dizzying phenomenon, I was completely befuddled by it, especially because I hadn't had anything to drink, not even a single glass of wine. So I couldn't help wondering if I was losing my mind — how else to explain such an obvious hallucination? Or if I might be having something like a stroke, or a brain hemorrhage, like the one that had suddenly killed my wife Kate just a few years before, or some other kind of dangerous medical condition — fleeting thoughts that passed through my mind much more quickly than the words I've just used to describe my passing thoughts. Passed in a flash.

By this point everything was happening so fast — not only the spinning and the rush of my thoughts but also my feelings of panic — that it seemed as if I had completely lost control of things, until suddenly, without intending to do so, I raised the index finger of my right hand in front of me, stared at the finger, and the spinning came to a sudden stop. I don't know what it was that moved me to raise my finger like that, except for some profound and irrepressible will to take control of the situation. Nor do I know even now whether the act of raising my finger and staring at it brought the spinning to a stop or whether it merely coincided with the cessation of the spinning. But I do know this: the whole experience, which probably lasted no more than a few minutes, was so terrifying and so exhausting that I quickly fell asleep without even thinking about it.

The next morning, soon after awakening, I drove myself to a nearby emergency room for a diagnosis of my condition, and after a battery of questions and tests, one of which involved being put in a revolving chamber, the attending physician told me that I probably had an episode of vertigo, probably caused by a minor problem in my inner ear.

Before I ever thought about writing this piece, the memory that stuck in my mind more than anything else was the spinning room — so much so that I didn't even remember having any thoughts about it. Beyond the spinning I remembered only my dizziness and the sudden gesture of raising my finger and staring at it intently until the spinning suddenly stopped. In other words, my mind was focused on the physical and visible sensations of the experience. But when I started to write about it, I began to recall thoughts that had raced through my mind in the midst of the spinning. In fact, the story of those thoughts and feelings turned out to be as important as the story of that hallucinatory experience. It's tempting, of course, to think otherwise, to suppose that the visible, audible, and palpable aspects of an experience are the most important things to remember and write about, partly because our immediate sensations are usually so strong—like the spinning room and my dizziness—that they dominate our memories, partly because we're so often told in writing courses to show rather than tell. But there's always more to experience than what visibly took place, namely what was invisibly happening in your mind during the course of that experience. And both aspects of the experience—the outer story and the inner story—need to be told, need to be interwoven, if you hope to do justice to the whole of the experience, particularly if you hope to convey a vivid sense of your self in the course of the telling. Imagine, for example, how different and diminished my story would have been had I told nothing about the thoughts that were running through my mind in the course of that dizzying experience.

Important as the inner story is in creating a persona, the telling needs to be enhanced as much as possible by elements of structure and style that can also bring your persona to life as vividly as possible. And that will be our primary focus in the next part of this book.

PART II
ELEMENTS OF WRITING AND YOUR SELF

Creating a distinctive persona involves decisions about a wide range of options, from the choice of a word to the design of a sentence to the structuring of an entire piece. So this section explains those elements of writing and provides exercises that will help to develop your ability and understanding in each case. Rather than offer an encyclopedic (and exhausting) approach to elements of style, I've chosen instead to focus on a select set of features that can make the most difference in your persona. This survey begins with four elements of composition that many writers consider whenever they begin work on a piece of writing—namely point of view, levels of style, organization, and continuity. These elements are so comprehensive in shaping your work and the way you come across in it that it's best to begin with them. Then I'll focus on types of word choice and sentence structure that contribute to a distinctive persona.

POINT OF VIEW

How should I present it? What point of view should I use? Such overarching questions arise whenever I think about writing a piece, whether it involves a memorable incident, like my vertigo attack, or an explanation of presentational strategy such as you're reading right now. If it's the story of a personal experience, something that I observed or was involved in, the first person singular, "I," comes to mind, for it's the most natural point of view to use with such material. And it projects the impression of a genuine and sincere persona. It's also the most intimate of the perspectives, so it's quite appropriate for a personal essay since it allows for access to inner thoughts and feelings, as you can see in these opening sentences from Nancy Mairs's "On Being a Cripple":

> The other day I was thinking of writing an essay on being a cripple. I was thinking hard in one of the stalls of the women's room in my office building, as I was shoving my shirt into my jeans and tugging up my zipper.

On the other hand, if you're writing a how-to piece or an explanatory work, you might do better to engage the perspective of your reader by using the second-person singular point of view, addressing "you," as in this paragraph and the following sentence about "how to tie a slipknot for kntting" from the Internet Web site, "Howcast":

> So you're staring at your un-knitted ball of yarn wondering, "What have I gotten myself into?" Fear not, a simple slip knot is the first step in any knitting project, so after this lesson you'll be an expert in getting started.

As in the preceding sentences, the second-person point of view suggests a solicitous persona, eager to be of help, and is particularly useful if you want to establish a more direct relationship with the reader than is possible in first-person singular.

The second-person perspective can also be used for personal stories if you wish to make a striking departure from the usual first-person perspective, involving the reader more intensely than otherwise. Suppose, for example, that I had begun my vertigo story like this: "Imagine how you might feel if the room started to spin shortly after getting into bed and resting your head on the pillow." An opening sentence like that one in second-person singular might draw you in more quickly than the one I previously used in first-person singular. Then I could easily shift into first person or move back and forth between the two in a mixed perspective:

> That's what happened to me a few years ago, and you can hardly imagine how it frightened me, for the incessantly spinning room made me think I might be losing my mind or having a fatal stroke like the one that killed my wife a few years before.

But perhaps the subject matter and purpose call for something that seems to be completely impersonal, such as the third-person singular, in which both one's self and one's reader are ignored on behalf of an apparently objective presentation, as in this sentence and the rest of this paragraph. This is the point of view that prevails in newspaper accounts, specialized articles, technical reports, and the like, which aim to create the illusion of objectivity by eliminating any reference to the subjectivity of the writer or the reader:

> The patient reported that his bedtime began as usual,
> when he lay down and rested his head on the pillow,
> but then it seemed to him that the room started
> to revolve, slowly at first, then so fast he evidently
> became quite dizzy from the spinning.

Now that you've seen how the presentation of an incident and the nature of your persona can change from one point of view to another, you should practice using alternative points of view by revising the first few sentences of your memorable incident in two different ways: (1) in a mixed perspective combining first-person singular and second-person singular and (2) entirely in third-person singular. Then write a few sentences reflecting on what you consider to be the relative advantages and disadvantages of each presentational mode.

}LEVELS OF STYLE

When you're planning a piece of writing, it's always important to consider the level of style that you intend to use, in order to make sure that you come across in a way that's appropriate to the audience, subject matter, and purpose of your work. A technical report calls for a more formal style than a personal letter, which in turn allows for a much more relaxed style. The difference between those two kinds of writing suggests a wide range of possibilities, but in general it's most useful to group them within three broad levels of style, ranging from formal to informal to colloquial. And if you're into short messenging services, such as texting and tweeting, you might want to add a fourth level, known as chatspeak, though the varieties of that are so numerous and complex as to require a separate article or book on the subject. So the remainder of this segment focuses on formal, informal, and colloquial styles.

Formal writing, as in this paragraph, prevails in official documents, technical reports, specialized websites, academic term papers, business reports, legal contracts, and scholarly articles. Writing for such purposes requires not only accurate and precise wording, specialized wherever necessary, but also complex sentence structure that reflects the complexity of information and ideas with which the writing is concerned. Given that the aim of such writing is to make an objective (or supposedly objective) presentation of the material at hand, the first- and second-person pronouns "I" and "you" are usually avoided in order to eliminate any hint of the author's being subjectively involved or attempting to manipulate the reader. Given the intent of such writing to appear proper and correct, as in this explanatory paragraph, it avoids the following kinds of usage: jargon, slang, abbreviations, contractions, colloquial usage, sentence fragments, exclamatory remarks, and sentences beginning with conjunctions or ending with prepositions. In other words, formal writing requires the avoidance of any and all forms of usage associated with a casual or colloquial style.

Informal style, as in this paragraph, is a bit more relaxed. You're free to write in the first or second person, free to use familiar rather than technical language, and free to use contractions, as I've done in this sentence. The general effect of such options is to create a more friendly persona, the kind of written self you're likely to find in how-to books such as this, newsletters, personal essays, opinion pieces, general interest/informational Web sites, letters to the editor, or blogs. But informal style is not so completely at ease as to indulge in slang or sentence fragments—maybe one or two for special effects, but nothing so extreme as you'll find in the next paragraph on colloquial style.

Colloquial style is where you can really loosen up. Loose enough so you don't worry about colloquial expressions like "loosen up." Or contractions like "don't." Or sentence fragments like the ones you just finished reading. Or street talk like "doing your thang." So it looks and sounds like you're just talking—letting the words come out in an easy sort of way. A way you can use in personal letters, personal essays, diaries, journals, memoirs, blogs, and stuff like that. Where you're free to make a sentence fragment out of a single word or two. For emphasis. Also to create something like the abruptly changing rhythms of speech. It looks easy, but it's no cakewalk—not at all. Fact is, I've been fussing over this passage as much as the formal one. Maybe more. Partly to make sure that every sentence or sentence fragment contains at least one bit of colloquial usage, the stuff that sounds like a person who's loosened up. No wonder Nora Ephron had so much trouble getting the hang of "writing that looked chatty and informal."

Now that I've defined the basic differences between formal, informal, and colloquial style, here are examples of each in three different definitions of vertigo that you might also find useful when reading the subsequent versions of my vertigo story. The first definition comes from the opening paragraph of Wikipedia's entry on the subject:

Vertigo (from the Latin *verto*, "a whirling or spinning movement") is a subtype of dizziness, where there is a feeling of motion when one is stationary. The symptoms are due to an asymmetric dysfunction of the vestibular system in the inner ear. It is often associated with nausea and vomiting as well as a balance disorder, causing difficulties standing or walking. There are three types of vertigo: (1) Objective: the patient has the sensation that objects in the environment are moving; (2) Subjective: patient feels as if he or she is moving; (3) Pseudovertigo: intensive sensation of rotation inside the patient's head.

As you can see, this is a clear-cut instance of formal writing that uses an impersonal point of view throughout and precise, occasionally specialized, language from start to finish. The definition in turn is methodically organized, beginning with a derivation of the term, followed by a notation of symptoms associated with the condition, concluding with a classification of the different subtypes. The collective result of the methodical structure and precise language is a very knowledgeable and systematic persona.

Here, by contrast, is a definition written in an informal style from the Internet site "WedMD":

Vertigo is a feeling that you or your surroundings are moving when there is no actual movement. You may feel as though you are spinning, whirling, falling, or tilting. When you have severe vertigo, you may feel very nauseated or vomit. You may have trouble walking or standing, and you may lose your balance and fall.

As you can see, this passage is more relaxed, given its second-person point of view, its use of plain and simple language throughout, and its use of complete but not overly complex sentences. It's meant for an audience of readers who might have had an episode of vertigo, like myself, and want to know more about the subject without being burdened by a technical approach. So the persona that comes across in this piece is much more genial and helpful than in the formal version.

And here at last is a definition of my own in colloquial style:

> Vertigo?! You might think it's fear of falling if you ever saw the Hitchcock movie. Dizzying heights and that kind of stuff. But it's nothing like that. Nothing. Totally different, like I found out last night when I got into bed and the room started spinning. And I didn't have anything to drink. And didn't look down from some way-high-up place. Just lying down with my head on the pillow, and the room suddenly spinning so fast I couldn't look at it without being so dizzy I wanted to puke. That's vertigo, as I discovered at the emergency room this morning. Something to do with stuff in my inner ear is what the doctor told me, or something like that.

From its opening one-word exclamatory query to its concluding conversational phrase, this paragraph exhibits all the features of a colloquial style, including the first-person point of view, the sentence fragments, the contractions, and the non-standard idioms. The resulting persona is very expressive and emotionally expansive. Yet within that expressive colloquial style, it makes an important correction of Hitchcock's famous but misleading movie that led millions of people to confuse the panic caused by a fear of extreme heights, known as acrophobia, with the spinning sensation known as vertigo that is caused by a problem of the inner ear. Based on the preceding examples and discussion of formal, informal, and colloquial style, I'd like you to write three definitions of a medical condition that you're familiar with, either from your memorable experience or some other situation.

ORGANIZATION

Organization, like point of view, encompasses the work as a whole, given its concern with the arrangement of events or topics — with what comes first, what comes second, what comes third, and so on. Such a structural matter might seem unrelated to the projection of your self. But if you think about it a bit, the way you arrange things will lead readers to form an impression, say, of whether you're systematic or freewheeling. If you want to be seen as an orderly and helpful guide in an explanatory piece of writing, then it's best to arrange things in a way that appears logical or sequential. But if you want to be seen as a spontaneous person, sharing experiences, thoughts, and feelings as they come to mind in an expressive piece of writing, then you might want to mix things up a bit, jumping from one to another without a concern for the logic of things. So the question of what comes first, what comes second, and so on, depends on the prior questions of how you want to come across and on what constitutes the most appropriate organizing principle for the subject matter and purpose of the piece.

If you're telling the story of a personal experience, the most natural way of organizing events is chronological, as in the first draft of my vertigo piece, beginning with the moment when I first sat down on the bed and concluding with my visit to the emergency room. Most of us, after all, are so accustomed to the chronological passage of time that we naturally revert to it when telling others about a personal incident. We begin at the beginning — or what we habitually perceive to be the beginning. But suppose instead that we were to begin in the middle of things, somewhat like this:

> The room was spinning so wildly that it made me think I was going crazy or having a stroke like the one that killed my wife a few years before. How else to account for such an obvious hallucination when I hadn't had anything to drink, not even a single glass of wine — when I was just sitting on the side of my bed, about to change into my pajamas? Just imagine what you'd think or do if you found youself in such a bizarre situation — so dizzy from the spinning that you didn't dare try to stand up for fear of falling down.
>
> It all started when I got into bed and rested my head on the pillow. The room started to move a bit to the right, then more quickly until the movement was so fast that the room seemed to be spinning out of control.

As you can see, I've inverted the chronology in this version, beginning with the story of my panicked thoughts rather than with the start of the episode itself. This rearrangement creates an element of suspense about the origin and cause of the spinning room, and it projects an impression of me, of my persona, as being at once panicked about the spinning but self-controlled enough to be concerned with the hallucinatory nature of the experience and thus with my mental and physical well-being. On the other hand, if I wanted to project the quality of a freewheeling storyteller, I might add a few digressive sentences at the end of the first paragraph, reminiscing somewhat like this: "The last time I felt that dizzy was seventy years ago when I got off an amusement park ride, called the Twister. I was just ten years old back then, eager for anything that would give me a thrill. And the Twister certainly did that, but it didn't make me panic anything like that spinning room."

Alternative organizational strategies can also affect the perception of a written self even in an explanatory work such as the second part of this book, which is intended to be very methodical. For example, when I first outlined the elements of writing that I planned to discuss, my topical outline moved step by step from the smallest to the largest elements of composition — from diction to sentence structure to overarching features such as organization and point of view. So I began by drafting the section on little words. But it soon occurred to me that while an arrangement moving from the smallest to the largest aspects of writing would be easy to follow, it would not take account of the order in which the elements often come into play in the process of writing and might have made it appear that I didn't have an experienced sense of the composing process. So I decided to begin with the large issues concerning point of view, levels of style, organization, and continuity that often take place early on in the composing process and then work through the elements of style that are involved in refining a piece of writing.

Given my experience in both the vertigo piece and

this textbook, as well as in other essays and books that I've written, the best way to start organizing things is to put them in the order that first comes to mind as being most true to the subject itself. Then, during the process of writing, it's important to remain flexible, remaining open to alternatives that might create a more engaging or compelling impression both of yourself and of the material. The same holds true for argumentative or opinion pieces. For example, it might seem most natural to begin by outlining your reasons for taking a particular stand on a controversial issue, but it might be more tactful to consider and respond to the arguments of your opposition before making a defense of your position, in order to show that you have considered other points of view than your own. Comparing alternative arrangements or alternative wordings is a useful way of discovering the most appropriate and effective form, whatever you're writing. So I'd like you to try out some alternative organizations for the story of your memorable experience and write a little piece reflecting on the benefits and the limitations of each rearrangement.

CONTINUITY/ DISCONTINUITY

The root of "continuity" is "continue." Thus the word refers to the quality of being uninterrupted and is such a fundamental element of writing that most readers take it for granted, expecting information and ideas to flow from one sentence to the next like the lines of type on a printed page. Such visible continuity is the sign of a writer in control of things. Most authors create that impression by focusing on the crucial elements of a piece, whether it's descriptive, narrative, explanatory, or argumentative. Focusing on an image, story, idea, or issue is the most common and effective way to create continuity, as in the spinning room of my vertigo episode. And it's best reinforced by dealing with related aspects or subsets of the primary subject, using details that are relevant to the subject and consistent with each other, as in the description of my dizziness during the vertigo episode or my discussion of focusing in this explanation of continuity. Readers are so accustomed to such aspects of continuity that any deviation from them will stand out, particularly if it involves a sudden change of subject or an unexplained shift in time or place, which will in turn raise questions about the intent and persona of the author.

"They're Kermits," she said, clutching the bright green mums as she bent over the dining-room table, poking them one by one in the metal flower holder. Though we'd just finished breakfast, Kate was getting things ready for our dinner party that evening, and she seemed as pleased with the name of the flower as with the flowers themselves. I had never seen such oddly colored things before — flowers the color of leaves — nor have I ever seen the likes of them again, but I can still see those mums in her hand and the smile on her face, still hear the pleasure in her voice, though ten years have passed since she told me they're Kermits.

Discontinuity such as you've just encountered in my abrupt leap from a discussion of continuity to the description of a memorable experience, is typically preceded and followed by asterisks, numbers, or space breaks, to indicate that the shift in subject is deliberate and purposeful — in this particular case to illustrate the element of surprise that arises from any abrupt change of focus. Contemporary writers have also used discontinuity as the basic form and strategy of pieces containing disparate incidents or observations that nonetheless are related to each other in one sense or another. For example, in the process of writing this paragraph on discontinuity, I decided to see if I could produce a set of variations on the theme of vertigo, to illustrate how disparate, discontinuous segments can have an overall sense of relatedness:

I was ten years old, and frightened at the prospect of having my tonsils taken out. So you can imagine how I felt when I was wheeled into the operating room and one of the doctors put a mask over my nose and mouth, telling me to count quickly to fifty. No sooner did I get to eleven than the operating room and everything in it was spinning and spinning, and the next thing I saw was a nurse smiling by my bedside, asking if I'd like a dish of ice cream. Such a swift and dizzying change of scene that I wondered if it was a dream.

On a midwinter evening, some five years ago, right after getting into bed and resting my head on the pillow, I noticed the room beginning to move a bit to the right, and then the movement increased, until the room was spinning so rapidly that I felt as dizzy as if my body itself had been spinning. Such a strange experience without any apparent cause that I couldn't make sense of it.

When professional skaters spin so rapidly on the ice that one can only see the motion of their rotating bodies, do they experience a sense of dizziness, I wonder, or is there a mental or perceptual strategy that they use to prevent it?

Though the earth is spinning ceaselessly in the course of its rotation around the sun, why do we never experience that spinning except in the alternation of night and day that transpires so imperceptibly from minute to minute that it seems as if everything is standing still, when in fact it's spinning so continuously that we should be eternally dizzy?

As you can see, I've incorporated the opening of my vertigo episode in this brief set of paragraphs that deal with other vertiginous experiences, as well as with questions about the relation between the activity of spinning and the perception or sensation of dizziness. Though the paragraphs are disconnected from each other by means of space breaks, and though each one has its own distinct focus, together they bear witness to my preoccupation with the phenomenon of spinning and its problematic relation to the experience of dizziness. Having written those paragraphs and arrayed them in a discontinuous sequence, I wondered what the effect would be of fusing them into a single continuous piece with an introductory statement as well as linking words and phrases, so I produced the following synthesis of the four:

From time to time, I've been at once surprised and fascinated by the dizzying effects of spinning objects. I remember, for example, when I was ten years old and about to have my tonsils out, one of the doctors in the operating room put a mask over my nose and mouth and told me to count quickly to fifty and no sooner did I get to eleven than everything in the operating room was spinning and spinning and the next thing I saw was a nurse smiling by my bedside, asking if I'd like a dish of ice cream. Such a swift and dizzying change of scene that I wondered if it was a dream.

More recently, on a midwinter evening, after

getting into bed and resting my head on the pillow, I noticed the room beginning to move a bit to the right, and then the movement increased, until the room was spinning so rapidly that I soon felt as dizzy as if my body itself had been spinning. Such a strange experience without any apparent cause that I couldn't make sense of it.

Given the dizziness I've experienced from the mere observation of spinning phenomena, it's impossible for me to understand how professional skaters can spin so rapidly on the ice without showing any visible signs of imbalance or dizziness. But that's nothing compared to my puzzlement over the fact that the earth is spinning ceaselessly in the course of its rotation around the sun, yet we don't perceive or experience that spinning except in the alternation of night and day, which transpires so imperceptibly from minute to minute that it seems as if everything is standing still, when in fact it's spinning so continuously that we should be eternally dizzy.

By contrast with the previous version, this one has continuity from start to finish and not just in my sustained focus on the relation between spinning phenomena and the sensation of dizziness, but also in the linking words, phrases, and sentences I've used to provide transitions from one example and one paragraph to the next. So in this version I come across as being more concerned with the problematic relationship, whereas in the discontinuous version the separate experiences and observations are more prominent.

Given the prior discussion and example of discontinuous prose, I'd like you to produce a discontinuous set of variations on a theme of your own choosing, incorporating some part of your own memorable experience. Then try your hand at synthesizing those separate paragraphs into a single piece with a strong sense of continuity. And as usual, write a short piece reflecting on how you were affected by those different modes of presentation.

LITTLE WORDS

Thus far I've been so concerned with large aspects of writing that this segment on little words might seem like a minor matter. But diction is the most basic element of writing, so it's bound to have a major impact on your prose, as you'll see from this segment. By "little," I mean words that contain only one or two distinct vowel sounds, such as "dog," or "work," or "ranch," or "water," or "campaign," or "little." Little words are the big engines of writing. It's very hard, in fact, to get on without them. Just give it a try, using only big words, and you'll see what I mean. Though some folks think they're small time, you can use little words to talk about the joy of music, the loss of a loved one, the thrill of a horseback ride, or a childhood friend, or the value of little words, just like I've been doing since the start of this segment. And you needn't worry about it sounding like baby talk or Dick-and-Jane prose. Here, for example, is a passage from the start of E. B. White's "Once More to the Lake," which has quickly drawn in many readers because it doesn't get bogged down in big and complex words:

> One summer, along about 1904, my father rented a camp on a lake in Maine and took us all there for the

month of August. We all got ringworm from some kittens and had to rub Pond's Extract on our arms and legs night and morning, and my father rolled over in a canoe with all his clothes on; but outside of that the vacation was a success and from then on none of us ever thought there was any place in the world like that lake in Maine.

As you can see, it's all in little words except for "vacation." Once you get the hang of it, you might find it a pleasure to see how nimbly you can avoid the big words and still tell your story or get your point across. It's a good mental game too, because it helps break the habit we all have of using the big words with Greek or Latin roots, many of which don't make as much sense as the little ones, the plain and simple ones that don't get in the way of what you're saying or thinking. Better still, when you use such words, you're likely to come across as a straight talker, someone who's not beating around the bush or trying to hide behind a facade of lofty words. So your reader is likely to trust you more, unless you happen to be writing for someone who's hooked on jargon or the big-time words that turn up in legal contracts and health care reports. The ones that leave you shaking your head, feeling locked out because you're not part of the inside group. I used to write that kind of prose myself, when I was a young man trying to get ahead in a world that favored the jargon of lit crit. But I never felt at ease when I was writing that kind of stuff, so I tried to get it out of my system by reading books and essays that favored plain and simple prose, then trying to produce ones like those myself. I didn't always succeed, but I did feel as if I was writing pieces that people could make sense of and might even enjoy.

As you might imagine by now, I'd like you to rewrite the piece about your memorable experience, using only little words. By telling about that experience in little words alone, you'll be able to see both the challenges and the benefits of using them in your work. Once you've finished doing your revision, I'd like you to write a brief commentary on it, noting in particular the problems you encountered and the satisfactions you experienced from recasting it in little words. Before starting on your revised story, you might find it useful to look at the revision I produced of my vertigo piece, all in little words:

It all began on a winter night some five years ago, after getting into bed and resting my head on the pillow. I noticed the room starting to move a bit to the right, and then the movement speeded up until the room was spinning so fast I couldn't sit still without getting dizzy. Very dizzy. I tried to resist the movement by looking at the dresser across from my bed, but the dresser too, like the picture hanging above it and all the other things in the room, was also moving along with the room.

Never having been beset by such a weird turn of events, I had no idea what to make of it, for I'd had nothing to drink, not even a single glass of wine. So it made me think I might be losing my mind, going bonkers, or that I might be having a stroke or a burst blood vessel in my head, like the one that had killed my wife Kate just a few years before, or some other kind of fatal problem working its way through my brain or my spinal cord—fleeting thoughts that passed through my mind much more quickly than the words I've just used to describe my passing thoughts. Passed in a flash.

By this point things seemed to be taking place so quickly—not only the spinning and the rush of my thoughts but also my feelings of panic—that it seemed as if I had lost control of things, lost control of myself, lost control of my mind, until all of a sudden without even thinking about it, I raised the index finger of my right hand right in front of my eyes, stared at the finger, and all at once the spinning came to a stop. I don't know what moved me to raise my finger like that, except for some profound will to take control of things. Nor do I know even now whether it was the act of raising my finger and staring at it that brought the spinning to a stop. But I do know this: that whole thing, which lasted no more than a few minutes from start to finish, was so tiring, so draining, that I fell asleep without even thinking about it, as if I must have passed out.

The next morning, soon after waking up, I drove myself to a nearby clinic in hopes of finding out what had caused my weird problem. And after a bunch of tests and questions, the doctor told me it was nothing to worry about, that it was almost surely a minor upset in my inner ear, a cold, or some fluid that had made my little world start spinning in a big way.

Before I started to revise this piece, I assumed it would require me to replace words of three or more syllables with shorter synonyms. But no sooner did I start work on the task than I found myself wanting to do a bit more, such as changing the first sentence to make the piece open with an air of mystery. And then I found myself wanting to add words or phrases or sentence fragments, such as "very dizzy," to intensify the sensations I experienced during the episode. And the short words worked so well to heighten my sense of panic that I made additions and changes throughout the piece, and you should feel free to do the same with your own revision. The only three- or four-syllable word that I was unable to replace with a shorter synonym was "vertigo," but the loss of that specialized word was offset by the gain that came from describing the cause of that condition in short and simple words that led me to conclude with an unexpected turn of phrase. I hope your revision will lead you into similarly distinctive phrasings.

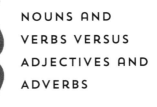

NOUNS AND VERBS VERSUS ADJECTIVES AND ADVERBS

Nouns and verbs are the workhorses of writing. Whether you're telling a story, explaining an idea, making a report, or sharing your feelings, the gist of what you have to say is carried by nouns and verbs. Try to communicate without them and you'll see what I mean. Without nouns and verbs, you'll be reduced to brief exclamations and queries, such as "Wonderful!" and "Why not?" With them, you can explain things, as I've just done in the preceding sentences, or you can tell about a memorable experience, as in the following paragraph from my vertigo story.

> After getting into bed one evening and resting my head on the pillow, I noticed the room moving a bit to the right. Then the movement speeded up until the room was spinning, and my head felt as if it too had been spinning. I tried to resist the movement by focusing on the dresser across from my bed, but the dresser, like the picture hanging above it, was also moving. And I began to panic.

If you examine the words I've used in this version of my story, you'll notice that it doesn't contain any adjectives or adverbs. The nouns, pronouns, and verbs are not modified in any way, because they don't need it. But I know how tempting it would be to accentuate the details with adjectives and adverbs, for I've used them in other versions of my story. And I've decided to include some of them here in another version of the paragraph you've just read, so you can see the difference between writing with and without them:

> After getting into bed one midwinter evening and resting my head gently on the pillow, I noticed the room beginning to move slowly to the right. Then the movement quickly speeded up until the room was spinning very rapidly, and my dizzy head felt as if it too had been spinning. I tried to resist the movement by focusing intently on the dresser across from my bed, but the dresser, like the picture hanging above it, was also moving. And suddenly I began to panic.

As you can see, I've added six adverbs and two adjectives, all of which might seem relevant at first sight, but none of which provides crucial information. It's not necessary, for example, to know the episode took place in "midwinter"; it's somewhat redundant to say the room was "beginning to move slowly"; likewise it goes without saying that a "dizzy head" would feel as if it "had been spinning"; and "focusing" on a dresser or any other object would by definition be done "intently." Besides, all of those adverbs ending in "ly" call attention to themselves rather than to the verbs they modify. So it's no wonder the novelist Stephen King was moved to say that "the road to hell is paved with adverbs." He might well have said the same thing about adjectives, but Mark Twain beat him to the punch, advising that "when you catch an adjective, kill it. No, I don't mean utterly, but kill most of them — then the rest will be valuable. They weaken when they are close together. They give strength when they are wide apart."

By following Twain's advice to use adjectives and adverbs in moderation, not only will your prose be stronger, given its focus on nouns and verbs, but your persona will come across as being forceful and direct. So I'd like you to rewrite a paragraph from your memorable experience without using any adjectives or adverbs. Then rewrite it again, using adjectives and adverbs only when you consider them necessary to convey important information that would otherwise be missing. Finally, write a paragraph reflecting on your assessment of these two different versions.

CONCRETE AND ABSTRACT DICTION

The nature of your written self is influenced not only by the extent of your reliance on adjectives and adverbs but also by whether your diction tends to be concrete or abstract. Concrete diction refers to things that exist in a physical, tangible, visible form, such as a weasel, a ribbon, an arrowhead, or a tail. A preponderance of concrete diction is likely to suggest a down-to-earth persona, someone who's in touch with the specifics of immediate experience, as when I tell about my dog who always lifts his leg on the same tree at the end of my neighbor's drive, or when Annie Dillard tells about her first sight of a weasel:

> Weasel! I'd never seen one before. He was ten inches long, thin as a curve, a muscled ribbon, brown as fruitwood, soft-furred, alert. His face was fierce, small and pointed as a lizard's, he would have made a good arrowhead.

Abstract diction, by contrast, refers to things that do not exist in physical form, such as beliefs, feelings, ideas, thought processes, and psychological tendencies. So a preponderance of abstract diction is likely to convey an intellectualized persona, as in this sentence from Suzanne Langer's *Philosophy in a New Key*:

The power of understanding symbols, i.e., of regarding everything about a sense-datum as irrelevant except a certain form that it embodies, is the most characteristic mental trait of mankind. It issues in an unconscious, spontaneous process of abstraction, which goes on all the time in the human mind: a process of recognizing the concept in any configuration given to experience, and forming a conception accordingly.

Though abstractions are by definition intangible, they are no less real and compelling, as you probably know from moments when you have affirmed your belief in something, perhaps with a placard in hand or a fist in the air, or when you've been roused to anger or joy by something that happened to you. So in a very real sense, one type of diction is not better or worse than the other, though handbooks and teachers have often recommended the use of concrete rather than abstract diction. Yet one need only recall a single sentence from the Declaration of Independence to recognize the importance of abstract diction: "We hold these truths to be self-evident, that all men are created equal, that they are endowed by their Creator with certain unalienable Rights, that among these are Life, Liberty and the pursuit of Happiness." Imagine how difficult, if not impossible, it would be to express those truths in concrete diction, and you can see that the choice of concrete or abstract diction is to a significant extent determined by one's subject matter and purpose. And the same is true of a related choice between specific and general diction. For example, in that earlier sentence about my dog lifting his leg, I could have referred to him as "my aged Welsh Terrier" rather than "my dog," and I could have referred to "the tree" as "the towering oak," but the specificity would have been superfluous and distracting. The challenge, then, is to attune your diction to the changing demands of both your subject matter and the persona that you aim to project.

Here, for example, is a paragraph from my vertigo episode, which I've revised to illustrate how the changing demands of one's subject and persona can lead to alternations between abstract and concrete diction:

> Everything seemed to be happening so fast — not only the spin of the room but also the rush of my thoughts and my panicky feelings — that it seemed as if I had lost control of myself, until suddenly without even thinking about it, I raised the index finger of my right hand in front of my nose, right between my eyes, stared at the finger, and the spinning came to a stop. I don't know what moved me to raise my finger like that, as if it were standing at attention, except for some profound will to take control of things — to stop the spinning room and to stop my spinning head.

As you can see, this paragraph, dealing with the climax of my vertigo experience, begins by focusing on my stressful state of mind, so the first half of the long opening sentence is dominated by abstract and generalized diction about "my thoughts" and "my panicky feelings," but the second half of that sentence suddenly switches into very concrete and specific diction, as swiftly as my attention shifts to the very physical gesture that I made with "the index finger of my right hand." That sudden shift from abstract to concrete diction, from general to specific, dramatizes the swift turn of events that I experienced at that moment. That sudden shift also projects the painstakingly reportorial and analytic persona that I aimed to project not only in the first sentence, but also in the retrospective and introspective mode of the second sentence.

To familiarize yourself with concrete and abstract, as well as specific and general diction, I'd like you to rewrite a paragraph or two from your memorable experience, expanding the material if need be to provide for opportunity to use all four types of diction in ways that help to project a distinctive impression both of your self and of your experience.

For a distinctive way of expressing your ideas and projecting your self, there's nothing quite like a well-turned bit of figurative language, also known as a figure of speech. Figures of speech use language creatively by altering either the literal meaning and/or the usual arrangement of words. The most well-known figures, such as metaphors, equate things that are not identical, as in "all the world's a stage," or "my towering oak is an air conditioner." If the metaphor is developed at length, it's known as an extended metaphor, as in these lines from Shakespeare's *As You Like It*: "All the world's a stage, / And all the men and women merely players: / They have their exits and their entrances; / And one man in his time plays many parts, / His acts being seven ages." If the equation is expressed in the explicit form of an analogy, it's known as a simile, as in "she put on her makeup with painstaking care, like an actress getting ready to appear on stage." If the equation attributes human qualities to animals or inanimate things, it's known as personification, as in "the drought has lasted so long that all the trees and shrubs are yearning for rain." And if the equation involves an exaggeration, it's known as a hyperbole, as when someone who is tired says "I'm dead," or someone who is hungry says "I'm starving." These are just a handful of the many figures, known as tropes, that deviate from the literal meaning or the actual nature of things.

Other figures of speech, known as schemes, rather than altering the usual sense of things deviate from the customary arrangement or selection of words. One of the most obvious but also most emphatic is an inversion of normal word order, as in "down the snow-covered slope slid he," which in this example involves not only a reversal of the ordinary subject-predicate word order but also another type of figure known as alliteration, namely the deliberate use of words that begin with the same consonant. Both of these schemes, like many others, are used for emphasis, as in anaphora, which involves a series of phrases, clauses, or sentences, each of which begins with the same word or phrase: "Down the snow-covered slope slid he, down the bare-faced rock below, down and down toward the end of his life." A few segments later we'll look in detail at some other schemes that can make a significant contribution to your prose style and voice, such as parallelism, balance, serial constructions, and periodic constructions.

The challenge in using figures of speech is to avoid ones that have been overused and thus are often spoken of as being "tired" or "dead," personifications that are themselves tired and dead. Better to make them up on your own, so they're fresh as newly fallen snow and just as vivid. As with any element of writing, the use of figurative language requires a sense of tact and care, as well as a concern for the purpose of your piece and the way you're trying to come across in it. Here, for example, is the paragraph about my tonsillectomy, revised to incorporate a few figures of speech:

I was ten years old, about to have my tonsils taken out, and I didn't like the idea of someone going deep into the back of my mouth with a scalpel in hand, as if I was the victim in a gruesome torture tale. Nor did I like the idea of being put to sleep with an anesthetic. So you can imagine how I felt when one of the doctors in the operating room put a mask over my nose and mouth and told me to count quickly to fifty. No sooner did I get to eleven than the doctors, the nurses, and everything else in the operating room were spinning and spinning, as if they'd been swept up in a tornado. The next thing I saw was a nurse smiling by my bedside, asking if I'd like a dish of ice cream to soothe my throat. Such a swift and dizzying change of scene that I wondered if I had died and gone to heaven, for she sure was an angel.

In revising this passage, my main intent was to give it more spunk by adding a few figures of speech that would dramatize the way I felt as a ten-year-old but also be in keeping with my present perspective seventy years later. So, given my childhood fascination with lurid mystery stories, I used a simile in the second sentence, comparing myself to "the victim of a gruesome torture tale" and another simile in the third sentence, comparing the whirl of everything in the room to a tornado, like the one I'd seen in *The Wizard of Oz*. And in the final sentence I used a metaphor equating the nurse with an angel in a phrase that's meant to resonate with the enthusiasm of a youngster. In each of these three examples, I organized my sentences so that the figure of speech would be located at the end of the sentence, which is generally the most emphatic, as you'll see in the segment that follows on sentence structure.

Using some of the different kinds of figures I've discussed in this segment, rewrite one of the paragraphs from your memorable experience or from your discontinuous variations so as to include a few of your own devising. Then write a few sentences reflecting on the challenges and the satisfactions you had in the process of doing this exercise.

Whatever you write about—whether it's the drift of your thoughts, a childhood memory, or a surprising footrace—your persona is determined not only by your choice of words but also by the grammar and structure of your sentences. The basic element in any sentence is an independent clause—a group of words capable of making a complete assertion in and of itself. To make such an assertion, an independent clause must contain at least a subject, such as "she," and a predicate, which is a word (or group of words) that makes a statement about the subject, such as "won." That basic clause, "she won," can stand alone as a complete sentence. Or it can be expanded in several ways: (1) by the addition of a word or phrase—"She won narrowly" or "she won, thanks to the last-minute stumble of her best friend"—yielding a "simple" sentence; (2) by the addition of a dependent (or "subordinate") clause, which refers to a clause that cannot stand on its own, because it's preceded by a subordinating conjunction, as in "She won, when her best friend tripped and fell right before the finish line"—resulting in a "complex" sentence; (3) by the addition of another independent clause—"She won; her best friend stumbled and fell right before the finish line"—resulting in what's known as a "compound" sentence; or (4) the short clause might stand alone as a separate sentence, followed by a longer sentence — "She won. The only problem is that her victory came at the expense of her best friend, who stumbled and fell just before the finish line." Though all but one of these variations conveys essentially the same information, the second and third are relatively understated compared to the first and fourth, which emphasize both the pyrrhic victory and the misfortune of the friend's loss, suggestive of a somewhat ironic and judgmental persona.

Other variations in sentence structure can be achieved by moving the main assertion from the initial part of the sentence to the middle or the end of the sentence, each of which produces a different effect, as you can see from the following examples: (1) "Just before the finish line, she came from behind to win, when her best friend stumbled and fell on the track"; (2) "Just before the finish line, where her best friend had fallen, she came from behind to win." In each of these cases, both of which are complex sentences, the emphasis changes depending on what is revealed at the end of the sentence, which is the most dramatic part of these narrative statements.

Variations in the length of your sentences can also create different impressions of your written self, as you can see by comparing the following passages, both in simple sentences: (1) "She won. She came from behind to do it. But her best friend stumbled right before the finish line"; (2) "She came from behind to win, her best friend having stumbled right before the finish line." The three short sentences in the first passage convey the same information as the single sentence in the second passage, but compared to that one they tend to produce a choppy declarative style, somewhat evocative of a young person. By contrast, the single sentence evokes a more mature voice, not only because of its greater fluency but also because of using the absolute construction "her best friend having stumbled," which is a more sophisticated type of phrasing than that of the first example.

As illustrated by this section, variations in the grammar, design, phrasing, and length of your sentences can produce different impressions both of your self and of the information that you're conveying. In order to get a first-hand experience of the differences, I'd like you to produce two versions of the first part of your memorable experience, one entirely in simple sentences of varying lengths, the other consisting of simple, compound, and complex sentences of whatever lengths you prefer. Then write a few sentences reflecting on the different effects of each version.

Here is the opening paragraph of my vertigo piece entirely in simple sentences:

It all started on a winter night, some five years ago, after getting into bed and resting my head on the pillow. The room began to move a bit to the right. Then the movement increased, spin by spin, sending the room into a whirl and me into an intolerable state of dizziness. I tried to resist the movement. I focused intently on the dresser across from my bed. I hoped that such an intense focus would somehow bring the spinning to an end. But the dresser itself, like the picture hanging above it and all the other things in the room, was also moving along with the room.

And here is another version of that opening paragraph, this one in a mixture of simple, compound, and complex sentences:

It all started on a winter night, some five years ago, after getting into bed and resting my head on the pillow. The room began to move a bit to the right, but the movement increased, spin by spin, sending the room into a whirl and me into an intolerable state of dizziness. Though my head was spinning, I tried to resist the movement by focusing intently on the dresser across from my bed. I hoped that such an intense focus would somehow bring the spinning to an end, but the dresser itself, like the picture hanging above it and all the other things in the room, was also moving along with the room.

This second version enabled me to produce a more fluent narrative. On the other hand, there's a tension and nervousness in those simple sentences of the first version that effectively suggest the increasing panic I felt in the midst of the experience. Given my differing reactions to each version, it will be interesting to see how you are affected by the two versions of your own piece.

Now that you've become acquainted with some of the basics of sentences, the next five segments will deal with various ways you can polish your sentences and your self, beginning with a type of structure that is useful in all kinds of writing.

PARALLELISM

Corresponding ideas expressed in corresponding form—that's the basic principle of parallelism. It may be as brief as a pair of words—"I adore and admire her." Or it might take form in a pair of phrases—"I deplore his greed and despise his grandiosity." Or it might include a pair of clauses—"He longed for her so much that he lusted after her." In most of these cases, the corresponding form manifests itself not only in word for word correspondence, but also in matching sounds in the corresponding words, such as "adore"/"admire," "deplore ... greed" / "despise ... grandiosity," "longed for" / "lusted after." The result is a forceful emphasis of the corresponding ideas and the projection of a self in command of language and ideas. Though the basic principle is quite simple, the stylistic technique of parallelism can be used in a wide variety of contexts, from echoing in a series of phrases within a single sentence, as in John F. Kennedy's inaugural declaration—"We shall pay any price, bear any burden, meet any hardship, support any friend, oppose any foe, in order to assure the survival and the success of liberty"—to recurring at the beginning of several clauses or sentences, as it often does in the Psalms—"He maketh me to lie down in green pastures; he leadeth me beside the still waters. He restoreth my soul: he leadeth me in the paths of righteousness for his name's sake." Indeed, it can be used to resound throughout entire paragraphs or sustain a theme through the whole of an essay or sermon, as it does in Martin Luther King's "I Have a Dream." As these examples suggest, parallelism is a recurrent feature of political and religious texts, not only because it compels the attention of readers and listeners but also because it highlights key ideas. And it is a vivid mark of eloquence in the person who uses it appropriately, because the capacity to select and arrange words in patterns corresponding to related ideas suggests the presence of a highly articulate and thoughtful person.

Parallelism is not only an important stylistic feature in and of itself, but it also provides the structure that is essential in other elements of style, such as balance, serial constructions, and periodic sentences, which follow. So it's especially important that you develop the skill of expressing corresponding ideas in the corresponding form of parallelism. Here, for example, is a version in parallel form of the first paragraph of my vertigo piece:

It all started on a winter night after an ordinary day some five years ago, after I got into bed and rested my head on the pillow. I noticed the room starting to move slowly, then more quickly, until it was soon speeding rapidly around in a circle. Such a rapid and ceaseless movement that it made me as dizzy as if I was spinning and spinning myself. I tried to resist the movement by looking intently at the dresser across from my bed. But the dresser itself, like the picture hanging above it, the mementos sitting on top of it, and the carpet sitting below it, was also moving along with the room.

In writing this version, I found that the necessity to put things in parallel form led me to focus more than before on specific narrative and descriptive details that I could itemize in balanced structures, as in the first sentence, or serial constructions, as in the concluding sentence. So I hope you will find similar payoffs by rewriting a paragraph from your memorable experience in parallel form.

BALANCE

With balanced form you can accentuate comparisons or sharpen distinctions between two related subjects, such as broccoli and cauliflower (both cruciferous vegetables), or Agatha Christie and Arthur Conan Doyle (both British mystery writers). If the pairs you choose have a common trait, each half of your balance will illuminate the other, whether the balance consists of two whole clauses, or it contains only two short phrases — brief as a breath, sharp as a point. As you can see from the two preceding sentences, balanced structure depends not only on expressing related ideas in parallel form but also on putting the parallel statements side by side, so that your reader can easily see them and readily hear them while reading from the beginning to the end of the sentence. Here, for example, is a sentence by James Baldwin that ends with a striking balance, as timely today as when he wrote it some fifty years ago: "The time has come to realize that the interracial drama acted out on the American continent has not only created a new black man, but it has created a new white man, too." The resonance of such a striking and insightful balance conveys the persona of someone who is judicious and thoughtful.

Balance can be used to heighten matched pairs of ideas, as in the sentences you've read thus far, or to dramatize opposed pairs of ideas, as in the maxim "one should eat to live, not live to eat." The balancing of such opposed or contrasting ideas is known as an antithesis, and when the antithesis uses the same words in reverse order ("live to eat" versus "eat to live"), it's known as a chiasmus—a word derived from Greek, meaning to mark with an "x" and thus to use crisscross arrangement. One of the most well-known chiasmic structures of recent times is John F. Kennedy's inaugural exhortation: "And so my fellow Americans, ask not what your country can do for you; ask what you can do for your country." One of many throughout the Bible can be found in Matthew: "Whoever exalts himself will be humbled, and whoever humbles himself will be exalted." As these examples suggest, chiasmic structure is a favorite of political and religious leaders since the verbal mastery that it projects is meant to inspire admiration and assent.

But balanced form can also be used in narrative pieces to emphasize important details, as you can see in this revision of my tonsillectomy tale:

> I was ten years old, about to have my tonsils taken out, and I didn't like the prospect of being knocked out by an anesthetic, nor did I look forward to someone going deep into the back of mouth with a scalpel in hand. So you can imagine how I felt when an orderly wheeled me into the operating room and another person strapped me down on the operating table. I wanted to run for my life, but for the life of me I couldn't run. Then one of the doctors put a mask over my nose and mouth and told me to count quickly to fifty, but just when I got to eleven,

everything in the operating room was spinning and spinning me into unconsciousness. The next thing I saw was a nurse smiling by my bedside, asking if I'd like a dish of ice cream to cool and to soothe my throat. Such a swift change of scene that I wondered if I had died and gone to heaven, for she sure was an angel, and her smile was a blessing.

In writing this version of my tonsillectomy story, I didn't want the balances to be so emphatic or self-consciously crafted that they competed with the forward momentum of the narrative. But I also wanted to see if I could include at least one chiasmus, or something close to a chiasmus, as in the third sentence, which serves to heighten my sense of panic at that point in the narrative. Now it's your turn to produce a paragraph in balanced form, either from your memorable experience or from your discontinuous variations.

SERIAL CONSTRUCTIONS

Serial constructions contain three or more phrases, or clauses, or sentences in parallel form. The parallel items in the series might be as few and as brief as the three short clauses in Caesar's celebration of himself: "I came, I saw, I conquered." Or they might be more lengthy and vividly detailed, such as the three verb phrases in Thoreau's celebration of a migrating bird: "The wild goose is more of a cosmopolite than we: he breaks his fast in Canada, takes a luncheon in the Ohio, and plumes himself for the night in a southern bayou." Or they might be as numerous as the predicate phrases in Samuel Johnson's gloomy reflections on human nature: "We are all prompted by the same motives, all deceived by the same fallacies, all animated by hope, obstructed by danger, entangled by desire, and seduced by pleasure." Or they might be as varied as the three sentences you've just finished reading in this segment, which together comprise a serial construction. Whatever their grammatical weight, serial structures tend to suggest the presence of someone taking a comprehensive view of things, as in Joan Didion's reflections on why she writes: "I write to find out what I'm thinking, what I'm looking at, what I see, and what it means. What I want and what I fear."

The effectiveness of a series is dependent not only on

the parallel form of its corresponding items but also on the presence or absence of linking words. In some cases, such as Caesar's "I came, I saw, I conquered," the absence of conjunctions, known as "asyndeton," makes his achievements appear all the more swift than if the last clause were preceded by "and," as in more conventional form. On the other hand, at the beginning of the third, fourth, and fifth sentences in the preceding paragraph, I've used more conjunctions than necessary (i.e., "Or. . . Or. . . Or. . ."), known as "polysyndeton," to emphasize those parallel sentences, which might otherwise be overlooked, given the verbiage that separates each of them from the others. A similar option can be seen in the repetition or omission of words in a series of parallel items. In Johnson's sentence, for example, "all" is repeated two times after its initial appearance but then is omitted in the later phrases by means of an "ellipsis," which refers to the omission of a word or words that can be inferred from contextual clues, in this case from the parallel form. Whereas in Didion's series, "what" is repeated from start to finish, emphasizing her commitment to writing as a mode of discovery.

No matter how long or short a series might be, whether linked or not by conjunctions, its sequence of assertions in parallel form serves to emphasize the corresponding import and interrelationship of its basic parts, as you can see in the following narrative of my tonsillectomy:

I was ten years old, about to have my tonsils and adenoids taken out, and I didn't like the prospect of being trapped on an operating table, didn't like the thought of being knocked out by an anesthetic, and didn't like the idea of someone reaching deep into my mouth with a scalpel in hand, cutting this way and that. But I never imagined that it would all transpire so swiftly, painlessly, and almost pleasantly. For right after being wheeled into the operating room, one of the doctors put a mask over my nose and mouth, told me to count quickly to fifty, and soon he and everyone else were spinning and spinning and spinning me into unconsciousness. The next thing I saw was a nurse standing by my bedside, looking down at me, asking if I'd like a dish of ice cream to cool and soothe my throat. Such a swift change of scene that I wondered if I had died and gone to heaven, for she sure was an angel, her smile was a blessing, and the ice cream was divine.

In order to produce the serial constructions that pervade this version, I found it necessary to expand the detailing throughout, with the result that this piece offers a more amply developed narrative of my perceptions, thoughts, and feelings than previous versions of the story. Also a more emphatic narrative, thanks in part to the ellipsis of "I" in the first sentence, which gives more prominence to the repeated verb "didn't like," and in part to the religious metaphor that caps the final series.

As you might imagine by now, I'd like you to produce a paragraph in serial constructions, either from your memorable experience or from your discontinuous variations. In the course of your paragraph, you should try to make use of asyndeton, polysyndeton, and ellipses for special emphasis, expanding your piece as necessary to allow for these special effects.

PERIODIC
SENTENCES

A periodic sentence, the structure of which derives from the grand style of classical oratory, is distinguished by the fact that its main point, its chief meaning, its central idea, rather than being expressed right at the start, as in a straightforward sentence, is not revealed until the sentence itself is complete or nearly complete. Of the various sentence structures we've considered thus far, the periodic sentence, thanks to the delayed revelation of its main idea, is the most dramatic. But if you're a no-nonsense person, if you're a straightforward writer and expect the same of others, if you don't have any tolerance for long-winded people — people who never come directly to the point, as if they were unable or unwilling to put first things first — then you will probably consider periodic sentences such as the one you're reading right now, as well as the ones preceding it, to be an exasperating test of your patience. Yet there's no question that the delay of its main idea — a delay that's long enough to produce a longing in the reader to know its specific import — endows the periodic sentence with a distinctive element of suspense, as in this sentence by Thoreau:

As the mist rolled away, and we were relieved from the trouble of watching the rocks, we saw by the flitting clouds, by the first russet tinge on the hills, by the rushing river, the cottages off shore, and the shore itself, as coolly fresh and shining with dew, and later in the day, by the hue of the grapevine, the goldfinch on the willow, the flickers flying in flocks, and when we passed near enough to shore, as we fancied by the faces of men, that the Fall had commenced.

In Thoreau's detailed sentence, as in my explanatory sentences preceding it, as in the one you're reading right now, you can see that the basic strategy of periodicity depends on withholding either the main clause or a crucial portion of it. In order to withhold the main clause as a whole, which I'm doing in this sentence and which is exemplified more flamboyantly in the third sentence of the preceding paragraph, the usual method is to begin with a few subordinate clauses. To assist the reader's comprehension over the course of such a long delay, as well as to make clear the relatedness of subordinate elements, you should use parallel phrasing wherever possible, as in the following sentence by Gretel Ehrlich:

Because these men work with animals, not machines or numbers, because they live outside in landscapes of torrential beauty, because they are confined to a place and routine embellished with awesome variables, because calves die in the arms that pulled others into life, because they go to the mountains as if on a pilgrimmage to find out what makes a herd of elk tick, their strength is also a softness, their toughness, a rare delicacy.

Although the periodic sentence has its roots in classical oratory, and thus might be considered most useful in political speeches and sermons, its suspended structures can also be put to use in explanatory writing, as you can see from the preceding paragraphs of this segment, and in narrative prose, as you can see from the following version of my tonsillectomy story:

> Though I was just ten years old and about to have my tonsils taken out, an ordeal that frightened me more than anything in my whole life, the question of exactly what would happen to me during the operation was, in fact, almost a total mystery. For beyond the inescapable reality that at some point a masked surgeon would reach deep into my mouth with a scalpel in hand, cutting this way and that — beyond that bloody, scary prospect — it seemed like I was embarking on something like a voyage into the unknown. So when I was wheeled into the operating room and one of the doctors put a mask over my nose and my mouth, then told me to count quickly to fifty, I had no idea that in doing so I would inhale so much of the anesthetic before I reached the number twelve that everyone and everything in the operating room would start spinning and spinning me into unconsciousness. When I awoke sometime later and beheld a nurse standing by my bedside, offering me a dish of ice cream, with an angelic smile on her face, I wondered if I had died and gone to heaven.

Now it's your turn to write a piece entirely in periodic sentences, based either on one of the paragraphs about your memorable experience, or on one of the thematic variations derived from your memorable experience. Then write a paragraph about the problems you encountered and the satisfactions you experienced in using periodic sentences.

}

QUOTATIONS

*Sometimes they stand alone like inscriptions on gates or
conclude like epitaphs on tombs; they filter through a text like
light through leaves or are enclosed like a hand in loving hands.*
— William Gass, "Emerson and the Essay"

No matter where they stand, at the beginning, the end, or scattered throughout, quotations lend other voices to your own. It may be the voice of a well-known person you invoke to establish a theme. Or the voice of an authority on the subject at hand to endorse your ideas, like a stamp of approval. Or a passage by someone whose words illustrate or exemplify your ideas. Or the words of someone who expresses your ideas more eloquently than you can yourself. As Montaigne said, "I do not speak the minds of others except to speak my own mind better." Whether you use them for assertion, validation, reiteration, or illustration, well-chosen quotations are a gift to your readers, offering them gems of thought and wording they may not have expected or encountered on their own. And the gift redounds upon the giver, for the presence of striking quotations in your text suggests that you are well read enough to have a storehouse of incisive passages at hand. And your text itself is enriched by the sparkle of other minds. In a former time dictionaries of quotations provided authors with a ready source of reference (and intellectual stimulation). Indeed, Winston Churchill believed that "it is a good thing for an educated man to read books of quotations." Before such collections existed, readers themselves kept "commonplace books," in which they recorded quotations that struck them as especially memorable—quotations they might later use in their own writing. So you might find it helpful to start a commonplace book of your own, though they can also be found on the Internet using Google. But no matter how you gather quotations, it's well to remember the cautionary advice of numerous sages when you put them to use in your writing—"moderation in all things."

To illustrate how a few pertinent quotations can brighten up a passage, I've expanded my previous reflections on spinning and dizziness:

From time to time, I've been surprised and fascinated by spinning things—and not just at penny arcades or amusement parks. I remember the first time, when I was ten years old and about to have my tonsils out, one of the doctors in the operating room put a mask over my nose and mouth and told me to count quickly to fifty. No sooner did I get to eleven than the operating room and the doctors were spinning and spinning, as if my counting had set everything in motion, like a nursery rhyme come true—"Eleven ships sailing o'er the main, / Some bound for France and some for Spain." The next thing I remember seeing was a nurse by my bedside, a smile on her face, asking if I'd like a dish of ice

cream. Such a swift change of scene that I wondered
if it was a dream or a wish come true.

More recently, on a midwinter evening, after
getting into bed and resting my head on the pillow,
I noticed the room beginning to move a bit to the
right, the movement picking up speed until the
room was spinning so rapidly that I felt as dizzy
as if my body itself had been spinning. Such a
strange experience without any apparent cause that
I couldn't make sense of it until a doctor told me
the next morning that I'd had an attack of vertigo.
Somewhat later, by coincidence, I read an article
about the author Laura Hillenbrand, who suffers
from chronic vertigo so dizzying she's sometimes
unable to read or write, and describes it as being
"like standing on the deck of a ship in really high
seas."

Given the dizziness I experienced from the
illusion of that spinning room, it's hard for me
to understand how professional skaters can spin
so rapidly on the ice without showing any visible
signs of imbalance or dizziness. But that's nothing
compared to my puzzlement over the fact that the
earth is spinning ceaselessly in the course of its
rotation around the sun, yet we don't perceive or
experience that spinning except in the alternation
of night and day, which transpires so imperceptibly
from minute to minute that it seems as if everything
is standing still, when in fact it's spinning so
continuously that we should be eternally dizzy. On
the other hand, I take comfort from the wisdom of
the Beatles' final press release: "The world is still

spinning and so are we and so are you. When the spinning stops — that'll be the time to worry."

As you can see, I've used only a few quotations, one in each paragraph, so as not to include more than the context will bear. In each case I've used the quotation for a somewhat different purpose. In the first paragraph I wanted to suggest my childhood state of mind at the moment when the sensation of the spinning room began, so I quoted the lines from a well-known numerical nursery rhyme, rather than acknowledging the obvious fact that the spinning was an anesthetic-induced hallucination. At the end of the second paragraph, I alluded to Laura Hillenbrand's description of her vertigo-induced dizziness because I wanted to reinforce the extreme dizziness I had experienced during my episode of vertigo. And at the end of the third paragraph, I quoted from the Beatles' final press release because I wanted to add a cosmic dimension to the piece by acknowledging the life-sustaining significance of the earth's incessant spinning around the sun. To see how the piece as a whole has been affected by incorporating these quotations, you might find it useful to compare this version of it to the version that appears at the end of the Continuity/Discontinuity segment. Then I'd like you to incorporate a few quotations into one of your previous pieces — either the story of your memorable experience or the variations on a theme related to your memorable experience. And write a paragraph assessing the effects of the quotations you added.

When I asked my editor how to wrap up this little book, her first piece of advice was "keep to your informal, confiding manner," and that's what I'm doing in this coda so you can see what's involved in sustaining a persona over the length of a whole work, right to the very end. And then she went on to suggest that I should remind you of all you've accomplished in such a brief space as this. So that's what follows, along with some suggestions for further reading and writing.

Now that you've worked your way through this book, doing the exercises at the end of each segment, you are, I'm sure, a more versatile and personable writer than before, capable of adjusting your self to the needs of various topics and tasks. I certainly feel that way about my own writing, having done all the exercises myself. The task of revising a paragraph or a whole piece again and again is quite challenging, especially when each revision calls for a different aspect of composition or element of style. Such a specific kind of rewrite, as you've probably discovered, is a goad to becoming as familiar as possible with the intricacies of each element and thus to becoming more knowledgeable as well as more versatile than before. It's one thing, after all, to read about levels of style but quite another to produce separate paragraphs embodying each different level in a definition of the same medical term. By the same token, it's one thing to read about the structure of a periodic sentence but quite another to produce a whole paragraph of them and then ponder how you come across in such an elaborate sentence structure. So while the various tasks might have seemed as artificial and demanding as finger exercises for a pianist, the agility that comes from doing them is mentally expanding. And the result is that your mind has become not only more adept at wording things one way and then another but also more knowledgeable about the effects of different wordings on the presentation of your experience, your thoughts, and your self.

Having acquired such knowledge and facility, you might well be wondering what's next. And, as with all skills, the next step is to take things up a notch, to advance to the next level of proficiency by means of additional reading and more exercises in one of the main areas or elements of writing that you'd like to pursue on your own. Given your personal and professional interests, as well as a self-assessment of your present writing skills, you are in the best position to determine where you need to focus your work at this point. To help you make that decision, I've prepared an appendix of suggested readings, grouped by specific areas and elements of nonfiction writing. The list is by no means exhaustive, but it covers the most relevant topics that will help you to keep improving your prose and the presentation of your self. Beyond that the only advice I have is to keep reading, keep writing, keep revising, and keep listening to what you discover along the way—from others and from your self.

SUGGESTED READINGS

MENTAL/SPIRITUAL GUIDANCE

The books in this area are oriented to developing mental habits and states of mind that are conducive to writing. So if you're inclined to feel somewhat uptight about writing, you might find one of these books helpful.

Goldberg, Natalie. *Writing Down the Bones: Freeing the Writer Within*. Boston, MA: Shambhala, 2005.

Lamott, Anne. *Bird by Bird: Some Instructions on Writing and Life*. New York: Anchor, 1995.

Moore, Dinty. *The Mindful Writer: Some Noble Truths of the Writing Life*. Somerville, MA: Wisdom Books, 2010.

TYPES OF NONFICTION PROSE

The books in this area focus on defining and developing skill in specific kinds of nonfiction writing, such as memoir, the personal essay, the interview, nature writing, business writing, travel writing, and so on. So if you're looking for guidance in one or more of these types, you might find one of these books especially useful.

Barrington, Judith. *Writing the Memoir: From Truth to Art*. Portland, OR: Eighth Mountain Press, 2002.

Gornick, Vivian. *The Situation and the Story: The Art of Personal Narrative*. New York: Farrar Straus, 2002.

Kidder, Tracy, and Richard Todd. *Good Prose: The Art of Nonfiction*. New York: Random House, 2013.

Kramer, Mark, and Wendy Call, eds. *Telling True Stories: The Nonfiction Writer's Guide from the Nieman Foundation of Harvard University*. New York: Penguin, 2007.

Lopate, Phillip. *To Show and To Tell: The Craft of Literary Nonfiction*. New York: Free Press, 2013.

Zinsser, William. *On Writing Well: The Classic Guide to Writing*. New York: Harper, 2005.

PERSONA

Only two books are available on this subject, and they focus on various ways that authors project themselves (or their narrators) in writing. So if you want to develop more skill in crafting a distinctive self, these are the books that will help.

Gibson, Walker. *Persona: A Style Study for Readers and Writers*. New York: Random House, 1969.

Klaus, Carl H. *The Made-Up Self: Impersonation in the Personal Essay*. Iowa City: University of Iowa Press, 2010.

STYLE

The books on this subject offer distinctive approaches to developing an effective prose style. So they are useful in and of themselves, as well as in connection with developing an effective persona.

Anderson, Chris. *Free/Style: A Direct Approach to Writing*. Boston, MA: Houghton Mifflin, 1995.

Klinkenborg, Verlyn. *Several Short Sentences about Writing*. New York: Random House, 2012.

Lanham, Richard. *Style: An Anti-Text*. New Haven, CT: Yale University Press, 1974.

Strunk Jr., William, and E. B. White. *Elements of Style*. New York: Macmillan, 1959.

Trimble, John R. *Writing with Style: Conversations on the Art of Writing*. Englewood Cliffs, NJ: Prentice Hall, 1975.

Weathers, Winston. *An Alternate Style: Options in Composition*. Rochelle Park, NJ: Hayden Book, 2008.

Williams, Joseph. *Style: Ten Lessons in Clarity and Grace*. Glenview, IL: Scott, Foresman, 1981.

SENTENCES

The works in this category focus primarily on the sentence, offering detailed guidance in the grammar, structure, and design of sentences. So if you want to gain more proficiency in the basic unit of English prose, you will find these books helpful.

Hale, Constance. *Sin and Syntax: Crafting Wickedly Effective Prose*. New York: Broadway Books, 2001.

Landon, Brooks. *How to Write the Kinds of Sentences You Love to Read*. New York: Plume, 2013.

Tufte, Virginia. *Artful Sentences: Syntax as Style*. Cheshire, CT: Graphics Press, 2006.

ACKNOWLEDGMENTS

Although this book is a distillation of ideas I've developed in my writing, editing, and teaching, I'm keenly aware of the people whose influence has shaped my thinking about the nature of a persona, elements of style, and various ways of showing people how to apply those concepts to their own writing. Professor David Novarr, late of Cornell University, comes first to mind, thanks to a graduate seminar of his on the seventeenth-century poet and theologian John Donne, the first half of which was devoted to an investigation of Renaissance English prose styles and their varied influence on the devotions, sermons, and theological disquisitions of Donne. Yes, it was a very specialized study, far afield from the basics of this book, but it was the first time I realized how a single author, devoted to the truth as he saw it, could write in such different styles as to sound like a different person from one work to the next. For that seminal influence I remain deeply indebted to Novarr. After that experience some fifty-five years ago, I developed a continuing interested in style-shifting, as the sociolinguists call it. So I put together an anthology, *Style in English Prose* (1968), to document the wide-ranging styles and ways of thinking about style in the history of English prose. So, too, I was influenced by Walker Gibson's textbook, *Persona: A Style Study for Readers and Writers* (1969), since its basic distinction between "writer-style" and "talker-style" gave me a fruitful way of introducing students to the idea of style-shifting as a crucial element in the creation of a persona. I'm also indebted to my colleague Richard Lloyd-Jones, whose writing assignments embodying rhetorical variations on a theme provided me with a model for writing assignments embodying stylistic variations on a theme. Likewise, I'm grateful to my longtime friend Robert Scholes, whose invitation to collaborate with him on *Elements of Writing* (1972) provided me with a model for the theme-and-variation method I've used in this book, thanks to his ingenious method of illustrating elements of grammar and style by means of doing grammatical and stylistic variations on the story of Tarzan, Jane, and Cheetah. For reading and responding to draft versions of the manuscript, I'm grateful to Jacqueline Blank, Trudy Dittmar, Brooks Landon, Anne Welch, and an anonymous reviewer.

Finally, I'm grateful to the University of Iowa Press and the splendid people who had a hand in producing this book, particularly Richard Hendel for his appealing design, Charlotte Wright for her meticulous oversight of manuscript editing, Karen Copp for her careful shepherding of the book through the design and production stages, and Holly Carver for her enthusiastic editorial support from start to finish.